LIFEBUILDER 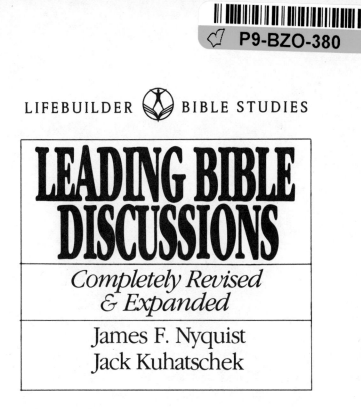 BIBLE STUDIES

LEADING BIBLE DISCUSSIONS

Completely Revised & Expanded

James F. Nyquist
Jack Kuhatschek

INTERVARSITY PRESS
DOWNERS GROVE, ILLINOIS 60515

20	19	18	17	16	15	14	13	12	11	10	9	8	7	6	5	4	3	2	1
99	98	97	96	95	94	93	92	91	90	89	88	87	86	85					

Contents

Introduction

Leading a Bible discussion can be an enjoyable and rewarding experience. But it can also be *scary,* especially if you've never done it before. If this is your feeling, you're in good company. When God asked Moses to lead the Israelites out of Egypt, he replied, "O Lord, please send someone else to do it!" (Ex 4:13).

When Solomon became king of Israel, he felt the task was far beyond his abilities. "I am only a little child and do not know how to carry out my duties. . . . Who is able to govern this great people of yours?" (1 Kings 3:7, 9).

When God called Jeremiah to be a prophet, he replied, "Ah, Sovereign LORD, . . . I do not know how to speak; I am only a child" (Jer 1:6).

The list goes on. The apostles were "unschooled, ordinary men" (Acts 4:13). Timothy was young, frail and frightened. Paul's "thorn in the flesh" made him feel weak. But God's response to all of his servants—including you—is essentially the same: "My grace is sufficient for you" (2 Cor 12:9). Relax God helped these people in spite of their weaknesses, and he can help you in spite of your feelings of inadequacy.

There is another reason why you should feel encouraged. Leading a Bible discussion is not difficult if you follow certain guidelines. You don't need to be an expert on the Bible or a trained teacher. The suggestions in this book should enable you to effectively and enjoyably fulfill your role as leader.

1
Why Study in a Group?

The study had already begun when we arrived. People were seated in a circle with Bibles in their laps. At first it was difficult to tell who was leading. Conversation crisscrossed from person to person. Everyone seemed to be involved.

The study that day was on the book of Jonah. We took our seats and were quickly caught up in the discussion. It was Darcy's turn to be leading, so she spoke up and said, "God told Jonah to go preach to the pagan city of Nineveh, but Jonah headed off in the opposite direction. How did God respond to his disobedience?"

We all looked down at our Bibles for a moment, then Steve said, "God judged Jonah for disobeying him." He explained that poor Jonah had nearly been shipwrecked, was thrown overboard, was swallowed by a large fish, spent three days and nights in its stomach and then was vomited on dry land.

Sandy agreed with Steve but felt that God was also merciful to Jonah. "After all," she said, "he could have let Jonah drown. Or he might have let him stay in the belly of the fish until he had been digested!"

After the laughter, there was a brief pause. "Anything else?" Darcy asked.

Curtis, who had been quiet up to that point, decided to join in. "God knew what it would take to bring Jonah to repentance. By the time he was back safely on dry land, and the word of the Lord came to him a second time, Jonah was more than willing to consider going to Nineveh!"

We went on like this for about forty-five minutes. Periodically Darcy would ask another question from our study guide. ("What was Jonah's reaction to the destruction of the plant?" "How does God's attitude toward the people of Nineveh compare with Jonah's?") Then several of us would respond, being careful to base our answers on the text before us.

Our Wednesday night group consists of a computer programmer, a homemaker, a marketing specialist, a publicist, an Inter-Varsity staff member, an editor and an artist. Darcy is a part-time secretary. None of us is ordained; only one person is involved in "full-time Christian work." Yet it was amazing how much we learned from each other. Each person provided a unique perspective on this brief but challenging book of the Bible. Together we relived Jonah's experiences. We felt sorry for him. We were amused at him. Most importantly, we identified with him!

We also got a fresh look at God, especially his care for people—even those we disapprove of. He lovingly disciplined Jonah. He had compassion on the people of Nineveh, even though they were part of a ruthless, idolatrous nation. His justice and judgment were unmistakable. But they were overshadowed by his mercy, love and forgiveness.

By the end of the discussion we were exhausted, but we had been stimulated, instructed and encouraged.

The type of study just described is a unique learning experience. Learning is often focused on the *leader* rather than the group. In a lecture or sermon the leader does most of the talking while the group listens to what is being said. Likewise, the leader gives all the answers and the group only occasionally asks questions. But in a Bible discussion the focus is on the *group,* not the leader. Since it is a discussion rather than a lecture, the group does most of the talking. The leader asks questions and the group supplies the answers by searching the book or passage being studied. The discussion then easily flows into real-life situations faced by group members.

This type of study also has a number of benefits:

1. *People learn how to feed themselves from the Scriptures.* Each member of the group is involved in discovering the meaning of the passage. For some, this kind of involvement is a new experience. They are used to being told what the Scriptures say. They may know a lot about the Bible, but what they know is the result of someone else's study, not their own. A Bible discussion encourages *them* to search the Scriptures. For many, the Bible comes alive in a way they have never experienced before.

2. *It encourages regular patterns of Bible study.* Group study is meant to supplement not replace individual study. Yet many people lack the discipline to study regularly on their own. A Bible discussion allows them to be involved in personal Bible study in a small group at least once a week.

3. *Everyone has an opportunity to participate.* Because the group is small (eight to ten people is best), the very nature of the group encourages them to be involved. They begin to realize that their contributions are crucial to the learning experience. Even people who might never share in a large group begin to open up. A small group seems more intimate, less threatening. Before long, many of them are talking freely.

4. *We benefit from other people's insights.* As each person shares, we gain a fuller understanding of a passage and how it applies to our lives.

5. *Participants become part of a caring community.* A group study provides a natural setting in which to get to know one another and to cultivate honest, open relationships. The members of the group pray for each other and care for each other in practical ways.

6. *You do not need to be an expert, such as a minister or theologian, in order to lead the study.* For example, it isn't necessary for you to know more about the passage than anyone else. There may be times when you will ask the group a question about a passage that you cannot answer. But with the help of the other members of the group, your understanding will be enhanced. Likewise, you don't need to be trained in public speaking. The group does most of the talking; you simply ask questions and encourage participation. You don't even need to be skilled in writing Bible study questions. There are a number of excellent Bible study guides available written by people who do have such skills.

Our group realized these things when we asked Darcy to lead us in studying Jonah. She had never led a Bible study. But with careful preparation, group participation and the help of a study guide, we had an excellent discussion.

2
Starting a Group

How do you start a Bible discussion group? Much like any group: you find people who have a common interest and who are willing to spend time together.

Interests differ from person to person and from time to time. Some people may simply want to find out what the Bible says; others may be interested in studying a specific book or topic. Still others will come to a Bible discussion because they are lonely and want companionship. Whatever the reason and no matter how varied the motivations, it is usually possible to find people who are interested in studying the Bible.

First Steps

1. *The People.* Think and pray about whom you would like to invite. You probably have certain people in mind already.

2. *The Interest.* Realize that a discussion needs only two people and that you may begin whether two or ten are interested. Also remember that an apparently uninterested person may desire to come just as much as someone who seems vitally interested. You may be surprised at who agrees to come.

3. *The Invitation.* When you invite people, you might say something like, "Ann, several of us will be getting together during the next few weeks to study the Bible. Would you be interested in joining us?"

Ideally the invitation should be made in person. But a telephone call, a poster on the bulletin board or an announcement at a meeting can also be effective.

4. *The Reminder.* If your invitations are given more than a couple of days before the study, a follow-up phone call the day before or a few hours in advance will be wise. If you're in a dorm or in a neighborhood, picking up those who've expressed an interest will almost always increase attendance and bring people together with a positive, accepting attitude.

5. *The Mix.* Caution: If you plan a study for non-Christians, the presence of more than a couple of Christians may thwart your purpose, unless they are loving people who do not insist on preaching to the non-Christians at every pause in the discussion. Group members should recognize that any person, Christian or not, is potentially able to make valuable contributions to the discussion on the basis of what he or she reads in the Bible.*

6. *The Plans.* Although you will want to announce the time and place of the first gathering when you confirm invitations, other decisions are best left until the group meets. This will give every member a sense that he or she is a vital part of the group.

a. *At the first meeting, decide on a definite time and place* to meet each week. It is usually best to meet somewhere with a comfortable,

---

*The remaining chapters will focus primarily on leading Bible discussions for Christians. For more information on leading discussions for non-Christians consult *How to Begin an Evangelistic Bible Study* by Ada Lum (IVP) or *How to Start a Neighborhood Bible Study* by Marilyn Kunz and Catherine Schell (Tyndale).

informal atmosphere. If you are meeting in a home, it may work best to rotate each month from house to house.

b. *Determine the length of the meeting.* A meeting can be of varying lengths: half an hour, an hour, but rarely longer than ninety minutes. Try to leave some time for other activities such as sharing and prayer before and after the study discussion.

c. *Decide what to study.* The group may be interested in studying an Old or New Testament book, character or topic (see chapter three).

d. *Agree on what you will do at the next meeting.* Who will lead? If you have decided to use a study guide, who will buy them? Will someone bring refreshments?

Our First Meeting

Our Wednesday night group decided to have a potluck supper during our first meeting. Steve and Darcy invited us to their apartment, and everyone brought something to eat or drink. The dinner helped us to begin relating to each other on a relaxed, informal basis.

After dinner everyone sat down in the living room. The leader quickly listed the things we needed to discuss. We decided to meet three times a month for at least the next six months. (It is usually best to set a time limit.) Each meeting would last from 7:00-8:30 Wednesday evenings. The first hour would be devoted to Bible study, and the last half-hour to sharing and prayer. We decided it would be nice if we always concluded our time together with dessert. (That has remained a highlight of our group!)

Initially, we agreed to rotate the studies from house to house. (Later, we found it worked best for a couple with small children if we met at their home each week.) We also decided what we would study and who would lead. We agreed to rotate the leadership so that everyone who wanted to lead would have a chance.

This first meeting went even better than we had hoped. And it quickly became apparent to everyone that a new group had formed since most of us were sick for the next two days with a mild case of food poisoning! (We still don't know how it happened.)

A Check List

The following check list can be a reminder as you begin to form a group.

Before You Meet

☐ Think and pray about whom you would like to invite to the group.
☐ Arrange the time and place for the first meeting.
☐ Invite people in person or over the phone.
☐ Advertise, when appropriate, giving the time, place and topic of the discussion.

At the First Meeting

☐ Discuss how often you will meet.
☐ Decide how long each meeting will last and how the time will be spent.
☐ Decide what you will study.
☐ Decide whether there will be one leader or whether you will rotate leadership.
☐ Agree on a regular place to meet.

3
Deciding What to Study

Once you have formed a group, how do you decide what to study? That depends on the group. During your first meeting, try to discover people's interests and needs. Begin by asking whether they would prefer to study a biblical book, character or topic.

But beware of one individual's pet peeves or pet topics. Select a study topic and format that will meet the needs and interests of the majority. And if a topic is too complex and out of your depth, don't be afraid to admit it. Request that you begin with a simpler study.

During the first meeting, you may wish to ask how the Bible has helped the people in the group. As they describe their own history with the Bible, group members will also have a chance to get acquainted with one another in more than a superficial way. It will also prepare the way for the decision about what to study together.

Studying a Book

Books are meant to be read from beginning to end. Can you imagine how confusing it would be to read a page out of *Tom Sawyer*, a line from *Hamlet*, then a paragraph from *War and Peace*? They wouldn't make any sense! Yet many people try to study the Bible that way. Book studies allow you to see biblical stories or ideas *in context* and to follow them from beginning to end.

If your group would like to study a biblical book, discuss which Old or New Testament books they are most interested in.

Keep in mind the needs of the group. If it consists of new Christians or people with only a vague grasp of Scripture, it would probably be unwise to study Ezekiel or Revelation! Stick with something that is easier, shorter and more foundational.

The book of Mark is a good place to learn more about the person and work of Christ. It is the shortest of the Gospels and is full of action.

Shorter New Testament epistles, such as Galatians, Ephesians, Philippians, Colossians, James and the letters of Peter, are also good choices. They are fairly easy to understand, and their message is basic and practical. For a leadership group, consider 1 and 2 Timothy or Titus.

Old Testament books such as Joshua, Ruth, 1 Samuel, Nehemiah, Amos and Jonah are popular. You might begin with something short, like Jonah or Ruth; then attempt something longer, such as Joshua or Nehemiah.

Studying a Character

Character studies can also be fascinating. Who can forget the stories of Noah and the flood, Abraham's sacrifice of Isaac, Joshua and Jericho, or Daniel in the lions' den? Character studies allow us to observe God at work in the lives of various men and women.

The Old Testament is a rich resource for character studies. Genesis, for example, looks at the lives of Abraham, Isaac, Jacob and Joseph. Moses is obviously the key figure in the book of Exodus. Judges looks at such people as Deborah, Gideon and Samson. 1 Samuel considers Hannah, Eli, Samuel, Saul and David. The books of Ruth, Nehemiah,

Esther and Jonah are character studies in themselves. The list could go on and on.

The New Testament also contains many interesting characters. In the Gospels you might consider studying Mary, the mother of Jesus, or Joseph, her husband. Mary's relative Elizabeth and her husband Zechariah also have much to teach us. Mary and Martha are popular for character studies too.

The book of Acts focuses primarily on the lives of Peter and Paul. But you also encounter such people as Stephen, Philip and the Ethiopian, Cornelius, Barnabas, Apollos, and Priscilla and Aquila.

The amount of information on biblical characters varies from a few verses to several chapters. A Bible concordance, such as Strong's or Young's, can help you find out how much the Bible says about a character so you can know how many studies to devote to his or her life. Discussion guides on biblical characters are also available at your local bookstore.

Studying a Topic
Some groups prefer to study a topic. Some basic ones to consider are evangelism, prayer and guidance. You might also study about Christian character, Christian disciplines, marriage, leadership, crosscultural missions or social responsibility.

The book of Proverbs contains a number of interesting possibilities for topical studies. You can study about the foolish, the wise, the simple, the righteous, the wicked, the scoffer and the sluggard. (See the Tyndale Old Testament Commentary *Proverbs* by Derek Kidner for references by topic.) Character virtues and vices are also profitable subjects. These include laziness, diligence, greed, generosity, anger, self-control, love and hate. A book like *Nave's Topical Bible* can help your group to come up with other ideas.

Studying with a Guide
There are several important reasons for using a study guide as the basis for your discussion, whether you study a book, character or topic.

One important reason is time. It takes a considerable amount of time to write a good set of discussion questions. Three to four hours per week is probably the average. Most discussion leaders cannot easily afford that much time in preparation.

Another reason is quality. The quality of study guides has been steadily increasing in recent years. Those who write these guides are usually trained in Bible study and have some expertise in the subject they are writing about. On the other hand, it is the exceptional discussion leader who has both the skill and the knowledge to write an effective study guide.

Study guides also allow the group to prepare in advance. We strongly recommend that each member of the group have a guide. Their preparation will greatly enhance your discussion.

What should you look for in a good study guide? Make sure the questions are clearly written, interesting and thought provoking. Good questions should generate discussion rather than simply call for one-word answers. They should draw out the content and meaning of the passage. Each study should also have at least two or three questions which apply the passage to daily life.

Be sure there are not too many questions in each study. Ten to fifteen are usually sufficient for a study lasting from forty-five minutes to an hour. It is best to use a guide which considers only one passage per study rather than hopping from passage to passage, though an exception would be a book like Proverbs. Also, does the guide provide leader's notes? These can be very helpful.

Fortunately, there are many excellent study guides available for you to choose from. You should visit your local Christian bookstore prior to your group's first meeting. Select several guides on various books, characters and topics. Most bookstores will allow you to purchase these on consignment; that is, you may return any of the guides for a full refund if your group decides not to use them.

Bring these guides to the first meeting. You might spread them out on a table or pass them around the group. This usually makes it much easier for the group to decide what they want to study. Once they have decided, you can order copies for each person.

Our group wanted to keep a balance among Old and New Testament books and character studies. We chose to study 1 Timothy for the first few weeks. Then we spent some time in the Old Testament, looking at the book of Jonah. Character studies came next, as we looked at the lives of Caleb, Gideon, Samson, Ruth, Elijah and several others—usually devoting a week or two to each. Then we concentrated on the New Testament book of Galatians. With sixty-six books and so many characters and topics to choose from, we have only scratched the surface!

4
Preparing to Lead

Bill was sitting in a large Sunday-school class one morning, waiting for the lesson to begin. The teacher of the class went to the front of the room and announced: "This morning we have a special treat. Bill has agreed to speak to us." A wave of panic swept over Bill as he remembered being asked to do this several weeks earlier. He had completely forgotten about it! Slowly rising to his feet, he went to the podium, his mind racing wildly. What would he do? What would he say? He quickly decided to talk on what he had read in his quiet time that morning. The lesson was not very memorable for the class, but *he* never forgot it!

Effective Bible study leadership demands careful preparation. Yet many wait until the last minute and then hastily throw something together. Is it any wonder that their ministry is bland and ineffective?

This chapter and the next two will give you the basics on how to prepare whether you use a guide or write your own questions.

Prayerfully consider how much time you should spend in preparation. A Bible discussion normally requires about two hours of preparation, although this will vary from person to person. This time should be devoted to prayer and Bible study.

Prayer

In John 15 Jesus gave us this warning: "Apart from me you can do nothing." Of course you *can* do something. You can carefully prepare and even lead an apparently effective study. But apart from the Lord, it will have no spiritual value. Paul recognized this fact when he wrote, "The weapons we fight with are not the weapons of the world. On the contrary, they have divine power to demolish strongholds" (2 Cor 10:4-5). The Lord is the only one who can demolish spiritual strongholds in our lives—those areas where we most need to grow. He is the only one who can transform our efforts from mere activity into life-changing ministry. Time spent in prayer is not time wasted. It is essential!

1. *Pray for yourself.* Ask God to help you to understand and apply the passage to your own life. Unless this happens, you will not be prepared to lead others. Charles Spurgeon, a great preacher of the nineteenth century, once wrote that he always meditated on Scripture "for my own soul's comfort—not in the professional style of a regular sermon maker, but feasting upon it for myself. I must know the preciousness of the doctrine in my own experience."

Ask God to help you understand the passage and the study questions so you will be able to concentrate on helping the group members learn from Scripture.

Ask him to fill you anew with his Spirit so you will be free from the self-consciousness that can so easily interfere with the work of God's Spirit in the group.

2. *Pray for the members of the group.* Think of them individually: their strengths, weaknesses, interests and knowledge of Scripture. Pray that God will enable them to discover something of the richness and challenge of the passage. Let Paul's prayer be your model. "And this is my prayer: that your love may abound more and more in knowledge and depth of insight, so that you will be able to discern what is best and may be pure and blameless until the day of Christ, filled with the fruit of righteousness that comes through Jesus Christ—to the glory and praise of God" (Phil 1:9-10).

Bible Study

Having immersed yourself and the group in prayer, you are ready to begin studying. Martin Luther compared Bible study to gathering apples. "First I shake the whole tree, that the ripest may fall. Then I climb the tree and shake each limb, and then each branch and then each twig, and then I look under each leaf." Here's how you can follow his advice:

1. If you are studying a book, start by reading it from beginning to end. This overview will help you grasp the theme of the book. Ask yourself how each chapter contributes to that theme. Pay special attention to the context of the passage your group will be studying. If the book is too long to read in one sitting, scan its contents, paying special attention to paragraph and chapter headings.

2. Next, read and reread the passage for the study you will be leading. Try to discover the central idea of the passage. Then ask how its parts contribute to that central idea. At this point your primary goal is to understand *what* the author was saying to his original readers and *why* he was saying it.

3. While you study, have a dictionary and a Bible dictionary handy. Use them to look up any unfamiliar words, names or places.

4. Once you have understood the central idea of the passage and how it applied to the original readers, think about how it applies to similar situations today. In what ways does it speak to your own needs and the needs of your group? What encouragement, counsel, commands or promises does it offer?

Do a thorough study of the passage before you begin working

through the study guide. (For additional ideas on how to study a book or passage, see chapter five.)

5. Carefully work through each question in the study guide. (If you are not using a guide, see chapter six.) Spend time in meditation and reflection as you formulate your answers. Philip Henry wrote, "A garment that is double dyed, dipped again and again, will retain the colour a great while; so a truth which is the subject of meditation."

6. Write your answers on a sheet of paper or in the space provided in the study guide. Writing has an amazing effect on the mind. It forces us to think and to clearly express our understanding of the passage. It also helps us to remember what we have studied.

7. If the guide you are using has leader's notes, familiarize yourself with those written for the study you are leading. Such notes are usually designed to help you in several ways. First, they tell you the purpose the study guide author had in mind while writing the study. Take time to think through how the study questions work together to accomplish that purpose. Second, the notes provide you with additional background information or comments on some of the questions. This information can be useful if people have difficulty answering or understanding a question. Third, leader's notes can alert you to potential problems you may encounter during the discussion. If you wish to remind yourself of anything mentioned in the leader's notes, make a note to yourself below that question in the study.

A seminary professor used to refer to the "parable of the peanut machine" (since there was a peanut machine in the basement of the library). The parable is very simple. You put in a penny and get a penny's worth of peanuts! The Bible says it this way: "A man reaps what he sows" (Gal 6:7). Good Bible discussions rarely happen by accident. They are the result of careful preparation.

5
How to Study
the Bible

Several years ago the *New York Times* ran an advertisement of Mortimer Adler's *How to Read a Book*. Under the picture of a puzzled adolescent reading his first love letter were these words:

How to Read a Love Letter

This young man has just received his first love letter. He may have read it three or four times, but he is just beginning. To read it as accurately as he would like, would require several dictionaries and a good deal of close work with a few experts of etymology and philology. However, he will do all right without them.

He will ponder over the exact shade of meaning of every word, every comma. She has headed the letter, "Dear John." What, he asks himself, is the exact significance of those words? Did she refrain from saying "Dearest" because she was bashful? Would "My Dear" have sounded too formal?

Jeepers, maybe she would have said "Dear So-and-So" to anybody! A worried frown will now appear on his face. But it disappears as soon as he really gets to thinking about the first sentence. She certainly wouldn't have written *that* to anybody!

And so he works his way through the letter, one moment perched blissfully on a cloud, the next moment huddled miserably behind an eight-ball. It has started a hundred questions in his mind. He could quote it by heart. In fact, he will—to himself—for weeks to come.

The advertisement concludes: "If people read books with anything like the same concentration, we'd be a race of mental giants."[1]

The Bible is God's love letter to us. But if we want to experience the eagerness and intensity of the young man in the advertisement, we must learn how to study it on our own. This chapter considers basic skills in how to study the Bible. Whether you intend to use a study guide or to write your own questions, these are vitally important skills to learn.

In order to read the Bible with understanding, we need to answer three primary questions: 1. What does the Bible *say?* 2. What does the Bible *mean?* 3. What does the Bible mean to *me?*

Answering the first question requires *observation.*

Answering the second question requires *interpretation.*

Answering the third question requires *application.*

Step One: Observation

Sherlock Holmes was known for his brilliant powers of observation. One day a stranger came into Holmes's study. The detective looked over the gentleman carefully then remarked to Watson: "Beyond the obvious facts that he has at some time done manual labour, that he takes snuff, that he is a Freemason, that he has been in China, and that he has done considerable amount of writing lately, I can deduce nothing else."[2]

Watson was so astounded by his abilities that he commented: "I could not help laughing at the ease with which he explained his process of deduction. 'When I hear you give your reasons,' I remarked, 'the thing always appears to me to be so ridiculously simple that I could easily do it myself, though at each successive instance of your reasoning I am baffled, until you explain your process. And yet I believe that my eyes are as good as yours.'

" 'Quite so,' he answered . . . throwing himself down into an armchair. 'You see, but you do not *observe.*' "³

The first step in personal Bible study is to make several *observations* about the passage or book you are studying. Like a good detective, train your eyes to see the obvious and the not so obvious. You can learn to do this by bombarding the book or passage with questions. Rudyard Kipling once wrote:

I have six faithful serving men
Who taught me all I know,
Their names are *What* and *Where* and *When*
And *How* and *Why* and *Who.*

1. *Who*—Who is the author of the book? To whom is he writing? Who are the major and minor characters?

2. *Where*—Where do the events occur? Are there any references to towns, cities, provinces? If so, look these up in a Bible atlas or on a map. (Many Bibles include maps.) If you are reading a letter, where do the recipients live?

3. *When*—Are there any references to the time, day, month or year, or to when events took place in relation to other events?

4. *What*—What actions or events are taking place? What words or ideas are repeated or are central to the passage? What is the mood (joyous, somber)?

5. *Why*—Does the passage offer any reasons, explanations, statements of purpose?

6. *How*—How is the passage written? Is it a letter, speech, poem, parable? Does the author use any figures of speech (similes, metaphors)? How is it organized (around ideas, people, geography)?

By probing a book or passage with questions, you will uncover many important facts. As you discover them, *write them down* so you can refer to them later.

The importance of careful observation cannot be overstressed since your observations will form the basis for your interpretations. In one of his most baffling cases, Sherlock Holmes commented to Watson: "I had . . . come to an entirely erroneous conclusion, which shows, my dear Watson, how dangerous it always is to reason from insufficient data."[4]

Step Two: Interpretation

The second step in Bible study is interpretation. Here you seek to understand those facts discovered through careful observation.

Were there any words you didn't understand? Define them.

Did the author use figurative language? This needs to be unraveled.

Were major ideas presented? Try to grasp their meaning and significance.

Did you encounter any difficulties? Seek to resolve them.

Meaning, significance, explanation—these are the goals of the interpreter. How do you reach these goals? And once you have reached them, how do you know you are not mistaken?

For example, have you ever been discussing a passage of Scripture with someone when suddenly he or she says, "That's just *your* interpretation," as if to say, "You have your interpretation and I have mine, and mine is just as good as yours!"

The person is half right. People often disagree on how the Bible should be interpreted. But just because there are many different interpretations of a passage doesn't mean they are all *good* interpretations. A good interpretation must pass one crucial test—it must conform to the *author's* intended meaning. You may have a seemingly wonderful interpretation of Scripture, but if it is different from what the author intended, it is incorrect.

How then can we discover the author's meaning? By following five steps:

☐ Discover the historical context of the book you are studying.

☐ Identify the type of literature it is.

☐ Get an overview of the book.

☐ Study the book passage by passage.

☐ Compare your interpretation with a good commentary.

1. *Discover the historical context of the book.*

The events described in the Bible took place thousands of years ago. This creates one obvious problem for understanding these events—*we weren't there!* Therefore, we often lack important information regarding the background or context in which these events took place.

For example, almost every New Testament letter was written to address a particular problem or set of problems: the Galatians were seeking to be justified by law; the Corinthians wanted answers to questions about marriage, spiritual gifts, meat offered to idols and so on; Timothy needed to know how to restore order to a church.

Unless we understand these problems or questions, the letters are like listening to one end of a telephone conversation. We hear what the author is saying, but we don't know *why* he is saying it. The same is true when we read other books of the Bible. We know only half of the story!

One way to learn about the background or context of a psalm, prophetic book or New Testament letter is to look for clues within the book or passage itself. For example, in 1 John we read, "I am writing these things to you about those who are trying to lead you astray" (1 Jn 2:26). As we look elsewhere in the letter we discover that these false teachers had originally been part of the church: "They went out from us, but they did not really belong to us" (2:19). John calls them "antichrists" (2:18). There are many other statements, some explicit and some implicit, which give us additional details about the situation that John's readers faced.

Once you have looked within the book or passage itself, it is helpful to consult a Bible dictionary or handbook. For example, under the listing "John, Epistles of" you will find further information about the background and circumstances of 1 John.

It is also a good idea to read related passages in the Bible. For example, Psalm 51 was written by David after his adultery with Bathsheba. We can read about David and Bathsheba in 2 Samuel 11—12. (In Psalm 51 the heading over the psalm tells us why it was written. When such information isn't given, a Bible dictionary will often mention related passages.) Similarly, if you are studying Philippians, you will want to consult the book of Acts, which provides information about the founding of the church at Philippi (Acts 16).

The more you know about the historical context of a biblical passage, the better equipped you will be to understand the message of the author. Such information can be like finding missing pieces of a puzzle. As they are put into place, the whole picture becomes clearer.

2. *Identify the type of literature you are studying.*
The biblical authors communicated in a variety of ways—through stories, letters, poems, proverbs, parables, and symbols. The *way* they say things adds richness and beauty to *what* they say.

The literature of the Bible has been classified into various types. These include:

a. *Discourse.* The New Testament epistles are the clearest examples of discourse, an extended, logical discussion of a subject. Some of the prophetic sermons and the longer sermons of Jesus also fall into this category.

b. *Prose narrative.* This is the style used in books such as Genesis, Joshua and the Gospels. The author describes and recreates scenes and events from biblical history which are theologically significant.

c. *Poetry.* The Psalms, of course, fit in this category. Poetry uses figurative language. It also uses different types of parallelism and is emotional in nature.

d. *Proverbs.* Proverbs, such as those in the book of Proverbs, are wise sayings. They are practical *principles* for living. They should not be confused with commands or promises.

e. *Parables.* Jesus used parables more than anyone else in Scripture. A parable explains a spiritual truth by means of a story or analogy. It is an extended simile or metaphor.

f. *Prophetic literature.* The prophetic books include the four major prophets (Isaiah, Jeremiah, Ezekiel and Daniel) and the twelve minor prophets (Hosea, Joel and Amos through Malachi). The prophets were spokesmen for God who announced the curses and blessings associated with God's covenant with Israel.

g. *Apocalyptic literature.* The books of Daniel and Revelation are a special type of prophecy known as apocalyptic literature. The word *apocalypse* means to "uncover" or "reveal" something which is hidden. One distinct feature of these books is their heavy use of symbols.

Once you have identified the type of literature you are studying, consult a Bible dictionary. For example, if you are studying the Psalms, it would be wise to read an article on Hebrew poetry in order to learn how it is put together. Likewise, if you are studying Revelation, read an article on apocalyptic literature. It will explain why this kind of literature seems so strange to us and will offer suggestions for interpreting it correctly.

3. *Get an overview of the book.*
On a large windswept plain in Peru, archaeologists discovered a vast series of strange lines covering an area thirty-seven miles long. The archaeologists first thought these lines were ancient roads. It wasn't until they happened to fly over the area in an airplane that they discovered their true significance. The lines joined to form a design, an immense mural that could only be seen from high above.

In Bible study it is helpful to get an overview of the book you are studying. The parts of the book only take on their true significance in light of the whole. But remember that the way a book is put together will be closely related to its literary type. An epistle such as Romans is organized around ideas. Historical narratives are put together in a variety of ways. Genesis (after chapter 11) is organized around people: Abraham, Isaac, Jacob and Joseph. Exodus is organized around geographical locations and events: in Egypt, en route to Sinai and at Sinai. The Gospel of John focuses primarily on several "signs" which Jesus did. Psalm 119 is structured around the letters of the Hebrew alphabet!

a. *Begin by reading quickly through the book.* As you read, try to discover its overall theme. For example, the theme of Romans is righteousness by faith. When it isn't possible to read the entire book in one sitting, you should try to skim through its contents, paying particular attention to any chapter or paragraph headings contained in your Bible.

b. *Next, look for major sections* or divisions within the book. For example, the major divisions of Romans are chapters 1—5, 6—8, 9—11 and 12—16. Each of these sections focuses primarily on one subject. Once you have discovered that subject, try to summarize it by giving a brief descriptive title to the section. For example, the various sections of Romans could be entitled: Being Declared Just (1—5), Being Made Holy (6—8), God's Dealings with Israel (9—11) and Living as Christians (12—16).

c. *Now look for subsections*—those major ideas which join together to form sections. The first section of Romans divides in two. Romans 1:18—3:20 describes the universal need for righteousness. Romans 3:21—5:21 describes how God declares us righteous through Jesus Christ.

d. *At each step of the way look for connections* or relationships between the sections, subsections and paragraphs. For example, Romans 1:18—3:20 is related to 3:21—5:21 because the former describes the *need* of humanity and the latter shows God's *solution* to that need. Other connections you might look for include things that are alike, things that are opposite, cause and effect, movement from general to specific and so on. Continually ask yourself how these paragraphs, subsections and sections contribute to the overall theme of the book.

In other words, an overview is like looking through a zoom lens. You begin with a panoramic view through the lens (reading the entire book), then zoom in for a closer look (identifying major sections), then still closer (looking for subsections). Now you are ready to focus closely on the paragraphs, sentences and words.

The more times you read a book, the more familiar you will become with its structure and contents. Your original overview will help you to understand the *whole* of the book. This understanding will tend to affect the way you interpret its parts. But as you gain familiarity with the *parts,* your understanding of the whole may need to be modified, and so on. Each time you go through this cycle, you will come closer and closer to grasping the meaning of the author.

4. *Study the book passage by passage.*

Once you have an overview of the structure and contents of a book, begin studying it passage by passage. In our modern Bibles a passage can be a paragraph, a group of paragraphs or a chapter. Realize, however, that the Bible did not originally contain chapters, paragraphs or verses (or even punctuation!). These are helpful additions to our Bibles, but we need not be bound by them.

a. Read and reread the passage in order to familiarize yourself with its contents. As you read look for the main *subject* of the passage.

b. Once you have identified the main subject, find out what the author is *saying* about it. If you are studying a paragraph, ask how the verses expand and explain the main subject of the paragraph. If you are studying a group of paragraphs, ask how each paragraph contributes to the main theme of that group. Do the same thing if you are studying a chapter.

c. Pay attention to the *context* of the passage you are studying. Read the verses or paragraphs immediately before and after the passage. Ask, "Why is this verse or paragraph here? How does the author use it to make his point clearer?" Keep in mind how the passage is related to the overall argument or theme of the author.

d. Notice the *atmosphere* or *mood.* Sorrow and agony pervade Jesus' experience in Gethsemane. Galatians 1 radiates the heat of Paul's anger toward the Judaizers and his perplexity over the Galatians. Psalm 100 is filled with joy. While this is a more subjective aspect of Bible study, it can give you rich insights into what the author or characters are feeling.

5. *Compare your interpretation with a good commentary.*

Once you feel you have understood the main subject of the passage and what the author is saying about it, compare your interpretation with that of a good commentary. It can give you additional insights which you might have missed. It can also serve as a corrective if you have misunderstood something the author has said. But do your best to understand the passage on your own before consulting a commentary.[5]

Step Three: Application

The ultimate purpose of Bible study is not simply to educate us but to *transform* us. In Romans 12:2 Paul gives us this exhortation: "Do not conform any longer to the pattern of this world, but be transformed by the renewing of your mind." As we renew our minds through the study of Scripture, the Holy Spirit gradually transforms us into the image of Jesus Christ.

To properly apply the Scriptures, we must remember the nature of Scripture. We mentioned earlier that almost every book of the Bible was written to address specific problems, needs and questions of the people living *at that time*. The Corinthians had problems of division, immorality, marriage, food sacrificed to idols, spiritual gifts and lawsuits among believers. Paul wrote 1 Corinthians to answer their specific questions.

We face many of these same problems and questions today. It is still

---

What to Keep in Mind When You Study

1. *Handle with care.* Study the Bible with the same diligence and care you would study for a test by a professor or a driver's license examiner.

2. *Assume the writer is being straightforward.* Don't try to find hidden meanings, but look for the clear teaching which may at first appear simple and obvious. We must learn the basic lessons the Bible teaches again and again.

3. *Use a contemporary translation of the Bible.* Among those which are widely accepted, the New International Version (NIV), Revised Standard Version (RSV), New American Standard Bible (NASB) and the Good News Bible (GNB) are probably the best. Paraphrases like the Living Bible and J. B. Phillips New Testament are fine for general overview preparation, but are usually inadequate for careful study, especially in the carefully reasoned letters by the apostle Paul.

4. *Let the material season.* Try to study the material several days ahead of time so it can mature in your own mind and so you can clear up any questions you encounter by talking with a friend or consulting reference works.

possible to take a fellow believer to court, and we still have questions about marriage. In fact there are hundreds of ways in which our problems and needs correspond to those faced by the people in the Bible. This is natural since we share a common humanity.

This leads us to the first principle of application:

Rule #1: *Whenever our situation corresponds to that faced by the original readers, God's Word to us is exactly the same as it was to them.*

But there are also situations from their day which do not have an exact counterpart today. This, too, is to be expected because of the differences between modern and biblical culture. For example, almost no one in our society sacrifices food to idols. In such cases we should follow the second principle of application:

Rule #2: *Whenever our situation does not correspond to that faced by the original readers, we should look for the* principle *underlying God's Word to them. We can then apply that principle to comparable situations today.*

What was the principle underlying Paul's words about food sacrificed to idols? He was concerned that the Corinthians not do anything that would lead someone with a weak conscience to sin: "Therefore, if what I eat causes my brother to fall into sin, I will never eat meat again, so that I will not cause him to fall" (1 Cor 8:13). This principle might be applicable to many situations today, such as whether a Christian should drink alcoholic beverages around someone who is a former alcoholic—or drink at all.[6]

Once you understand these principles of application, you can think of unlimited ways in which God's Word applies today. You can ask such questions as:

☐ Is there a command for me to obey?

☐ Is there a promise to claim?

☐ Is there an example to follow?

☐ Is there a sin to avoid or confess?

☐ Is there a reason for thanksgiving or praise?

☐ What does this passage teach me about God, Jesus, myself, others?

When you have completed your observation, interpretation and application of a passage, you can then finish steps 5-7 described on page 23 in the last chapter. If you are writing your own questions for the discussion, follow the suggestions found in the next chapter.

Practice Makes Perfect (Well, Almost)

Learning to study the Bible is like learning any other skill—the more you do it, the easier it becomes. At first, following the steps outlined in this chapter may seem mechanical, like learning how to type. But after a while, many of these steps will seem much more natural, almost automatic. And remember, you are not alone in Bible study. The Holy Spirit did not write Scripture in order to confuse us. He will help you to understand and apply the Bible as you pray, study diligently and make use of many of the study aids available today. Bon appetit!

[1]As quoted by Robert A. Traina, *Methodical Bible Study* (Wilmore, Ky.: Asbury Theological Seminary, 1952), pp. 97-98.
[2]*The Illustrated Sherlock Holmes Treasury* (New York: Avenel Books, 1976), p. 17.
[3]Ibid., p. 2 (emphasis added).
[4]Ibid., p. 112.
[5]An excellent introduction to the basic principles of interpreting Scripture is T. Norton Sterrett, *How to Understand Your Bible* (Downers Grove, Ill.: InterVarsity Press, 1974).
[6]The principles of application are more fully explained by Douglas Stuart and Gordon Fee in *How to Read the Bible for All Its Worth* (Grand Rapids, Mich.: Zondervan, 1982), pp. 57-71. This is an excellent book on Bible study.

6
How to Write Questions

Good questions are the keys which unlock a passage. They help us to observe what it says, interpret its meaning and apply what we learn. Good questions are also like the baton in the hand of a symphony conductor. They assure that people follow the music and work together harmoniously.

Chapter three suggested using a study guide when leading a discussion. There may be times, however, when you desire to write your own questions. A good study guide may not be available for the book or topic you have chosen. Or you may wish to write a study directed to the specific needs of your group.

Even with a study guide it is helpful to know how to form questions. For one thing, when a vigorous discussion wanders off course, you can ask follow-up questions to keep the discussion moving constructively. Also, you will be able to personalize questions from the study guide to suit your group.

This chapter can help you write good questions and put them together into a well-organized, effective study. We will actually take you through the process of writing a study based on Matthew 20:20-28:

Then the mother of Zebedee's sons came to Jesus with her sons and, kneeling down, asked a favor of him.

"What is it you want?" he asked.

She said, "Grant that one of these two sons of mine may sit at your right and the other at your left in your kingdom."

"You don't know what you are asking," Jesus said to them. "Can you drink the cup I am going to drink?"

"We can," they answered.

Jesus said to them, "You will indeed drink from my cup, but to sit at my right or left is not for me to grant. These places belong to those for whom they have been prepared by my Father."

When the ten heard about this, they were indignant with the two brothers. Jesus called them together and said, "You know that the rulers of the Gentiles lord it over them, and their high officials exercise authority over them. Not so with you. Instead, whoever wants to become great among you must be your servant, and whoever wants to be first must be your slave—just as the Son of man did not come to be served, but to serve, and to give his life as a ransom for many."

The Aim of the Study

It has been said, "If you aim at nothing, you'll hit it every time." How true! A good study should have a clearly defined purpose. Once you have studied the passage on your own, form a statement of purpose for the study based on the primary focus of the passage. For example, in the passage above, since Jesus focuses on the meaning of greatness, your purpose statement might be: "The purpose of this study is to learn the true meaning of greatness." Decide the purpose *before* writing your study so that the questions will reflect that purpose.

Introducing the Study

An introduction can set the tone for the entire study. Your purpose statement can serve as a natural theme for these opening remarks.

A good introduction should have three characteristics: *First,* it should be *interesting.* At the beginning of a study, people's minds are usually wandering. A good introduction should grab their attention.

Second, a good introduction should *expose a need.* If people feel that the passage will be speaking to a real concern or lack in their lives, they will be much more eager to study it.

Third, a good introduction should *orient* the group to the passage being studied. It should briefly describe the subject of the passage and how that subject relates to the needs of the group.

If we keep these goals in mind, an introduction for Matthew 20 might be as follows:

Power, glory, success. These are the marks of greatness in our so- ciety. People want to be at the top, to see their name in lights, to bathe themselves in luxury. When measured by these standards, few of us achieve greatness. But in Matthew 20 Jesus stands the world's concept of greatness on its head. He also offers us a chance to become truly great.

Types of Questions

As you begin writing the questions for your study, it is important to realize there are several types of questions:

1. *Approach questions.* An approach question is asked at the begin- ning of the study *before* the passage is read. It can spark a discussion in three ways:

First, it helps the group members to warm up to each other. No matter how well people may know each other or how comfortable they may be with each other, there is always a stiffness that needs to be overcome before people will begin to talk openly. An approach ques- tion helps to break the ice. For example, in this study on Matthew 20 we might ask: "When you were a child, what did you want to be when you grew up?"

Second, an approach question gets people thinking along the lines of the topic of the study. Most people will have lots of different things going on in their minds (dinner, an important meeting coming up, how to get the car fixed) that will have nothing to do with the study. A creative question will get their attention and draw them into the discussion.

Third, an approach question can reveal where our thoughts or feelings need to be transformed by Scripture. This is why it is especially important *not* to read the passage before the approach question is asked. The passage will tend to color the honest reactions people would otherwise give because they are of course *supposed* to think the way the Bible does. Giving honest responses to various issues before they find out what the Bible says may help them see where their thoughts or attitudes need to be changed. For example, in our study we might ask: "Do you feel successful? Explain why or why not."

2. *Observation questions.* As you studied the passage on your own, you *observed* many important facts related to who, what, when, where, why and how (see chapter five). Some of these facts were more significant than others in helping you to interpret and apply the passage. Now you want to help the group to observe these significant facts. *Do this by turning your observations into questions.* For example, in Matthew 20 the following observations are likely candidates for questions:

Observation: The main characters in this passage are Jesus, the mother, her two sons and the other ten disciples.
Question: Who are the main characters in this passage?

Observation: The mother asks Jesus to allow her two sons to sit on his right and left in his kingdom.
Question: What favor does the mother ask of Jesus?

Observation: Jesus states that the Gentiles define greatness as having others serve you. He defines greatness as you serving others.
Question: What definitions of greatness does Jesus give in this passage?

Good observation questions should cause the group to search the passage and its context. They should not be so simple or superficial that they can be answered with one- or two-word answers.

3. *Interpretation questions.* After you observed the facts of the passage in your own study, you sought to *interpret* the meaning and significance of those facts. You began to understand the main point of the passage and how the parts of the passage contribute to that main point. Now you want to lead the group to understand what the passage means.

Do this by turning significant interpretations into questions. (Caution: Be sure your questions allow the group the freedom to arrive at their own interpretations, even if their views differ from yours.) The following examples from Matthew 20 illustrate how you might do this:

> *Interpretation:* The seats on the right and left of a host were positions of honor. The two sons wanted the second and third highest positions in the kingdom.
> *Question:* What would be the significance of sitting on Jesus' right and left hand in his kingdom?

> *Interpretation:* Jesus uses the word *cup* as a metaphor for suffering, especially the suffering which leads to death. Jesus would die, as would the two sons as a result of their close following of him.
> *Question:* What is the "cup" from which Jesus and the two sons will drink?

> *Interpretation:* The ten disciples were indignant because *they* wanted the highest positions in the kingdom but the two sons had tried to get to Jesus first.
> *Question:* Why do you think the ten disciples were indignant toward the other two?

4. *Application questions.* After you observed and interpreted the passage in your own study, you also sought to *apply* it to your life. Through careful reflection and prayer, you saw how your attitudes, relationships and actions should begin to change. Now you need to help the group to think about how they should apply what they have observed and interpreted.

Do this by turning some of your applications into questions. But be sure that the questions are flexible enough to allow the main idea of the passage to be applied in a variety of ways. For example, in the Matthew 20 passage you might do this:

> *Application:* This passage should begin to affect the way I treat my family, the

people at work and those who live around me. For example, at home I should be more willing to do those jobs which no one else likes to do, such as washing dishes and carrying out the trash.

Question: How can you serve those around you in your family, at work or school, in society?

Application: I should begin cultivating the attitude of a servant this week. I will volunteer to do the dinner dishes at least twice this week.

Question: What specific act of service can you do for someone this week?

Application: If I demonstrate a willingness to do menial tasks, others might start giving me the jobs that no one else wants to do. They might take unfair advantage of me, just as I have previously taken unfair advantage of others.

Question: If you seek to become a servant to others, what difficulties might you encounter?

Application questions should be closely related to the main points of the passage. It is better to have three or four scattered throughout the study than simply one or two at the end.

5. *Overview and summary questions.* An overview question allows the group to view a passage or book as a whole before they study its parts. A summary question helps to draw together the main points of a passage or book after they have been studied.

a. *Overview:* Try to visualize the people and the setting in Matthew 20:20-28. Describe what you see.

b. *Summary:* What has this passage taught us about the true meaning of greatness?

6. *Combination questions.* Sometimes it is best to have a question which serves more than one purpose. These often generate more discussion than a simple observation or interpretation question.

For example, a question can combine observation with interpretation: "Why do you think the ten disciples responded as they did toward the other two?" (This question requires the group to observe *how* the disciples responded, but also asks them to think about *why.*) Or the question may make an observation and then follow it with an interpretation or application question: "Jesus states that he did not come to be served but to serve. How can you follow his example this week?"

Also, you may preface a question with important background information: "The seats on the right and left of a host were positions of honor. How does this help us to understand the mother's request?" Such questions are often more efficient than those which maintain a rigid distinction between observation, interpretation and application. They also help to give direction to the study.

Organizing Your Questions

After you have written your questions, you will want to make your final organization. Try to begin with your introduction, followed by the approach question, followed by reading the passage. Now arrange the rest of your questions. You could put all your observation questions first, followed by all your interpretation questions and end with your application questions. For some passages of Scripture, this may be the most natural approach. But a study is usually more interesting if you mix the various kinds of questions, basically repeating the observa-

---

Structuring a Study

Example 1
1. Introduction
2. Approach question
3. Reading the passage
4. Observation question
5. Observation question
6. Observation question
7. Observation question
8. Interpretation question
9. Interpretation question
10. Interpretation question
11. Application question
12. Application question

Example 2
1. Introduction
2. Approach question
3. Reading the passage
4. Observation question
5. Interpretation question
6. Combination observation/ interpretation question
7. Application question
8. Observation question
9. Interpretation question
10. Application question
11. Combination observation/ interpretation question
12. Interpretation question
13. Interpretation question
14. Application question
15. Summary question

tion/interpretation/application pattern.

Also consider which questions are absolutely crucial to ask. Put a star or check mark by these so you can be sure to ask them if time begins to run short. Considering in advance various ways to shorten a study may give you a lot more ease as a leader in the second half of the study.

Evaluating Your Questions

Writing good questions requires thought, patience and skill. Like any other skill, your ability will improve with practice. Once you have completed your study questions, ask yourself whether they have the following characteristics:

1. Your questions should be clear. If some are not, try rewording them.

2. Your questions should not be too long or complex. Those which are should be broken into separate questions.

3. Your questions should generate discussion. If any can be answered with a yes, no or other one-word answer, try to make them more challenging.

4. Your questions should cause the group to search the text.

5. Your questions should move the group through the passage in a logical sequence.

6. They should draw out and apply the main points of the passage.

7. They should usually be related to one passage rather than asking the group to jump from book to book or passage to passage.

8. There should be a proper number of questions for the time allotted to the study. Usually twelve to fifteen questions are sufficient for a one-hour study.

In addition to evaluating individual questions, look at the study as a whole.

☐ Do the questions flow harmoniously?

☐ Do they follow the general sequence of observation, interpretation and application? (This pattern may occur more than once in the study.)

☐ Is there a proper balance among these three types of questions?

☐ Does each question lead naturally into the next?

□ Does the study achieve the purpose you worked out initially?

The best way to evaluate the questions you have written is in an actual group discussion. Sometimes a question which looks good on paper may not work in a group. Likewise, some seemingly ordinary questions may do an excellent job of generating discussion. It is a good idea, then, to evaluate your questions again at the end of the study. Use the evaluation guide in chapter eight. The feedback you receive from the group should help you to improve the quality of your questions in the future.

Evaluating Discussion Questions

Here are some examples of questions to clarify what we've been saying about the strengths and weaknesses of several questions. Consider Luke 4:38-39: "Jesus left the synagogue and went to the home of Simon. Now Simon's mother-in-law was suffering from a high fever, and they asked Jesus to help her. So he bent over her and rebuked the fever, and it left her: she got up at once and began to wait on them."

Observation Questions	*Evaluation*
1a. Who are the characters in this incident?	This forces the group to look at the entire section. But it might better be put in simpler terms, as in 1b.
1b. Who are the people in this story?	A clearer way of putting 1a.
1c. Describe the people in this story.	The word *describe* stimulates a more extensive searching of the text than the simple word *who* and should encourage broader discussion.
2a. Was Simon's mother-in-law ill?	This one-word answer, yes, may be considered too simple and obvious. It doesn't provoke much thought.
2b. What happened to the fever?	Same problems as question 2a.
2c. What did each person in the story do?	Stimulates searching of the text and allows several members to respond.
3a. How did Jesus affect the different people in this story?	This question highlights Jesus as the center of the story, and fits in with the purpose of Luke, the author.
3b. What does this story teach us about Jesus?	More comprehensive than 3a and allows the group to think about any aspect of Jesus that the story covers.

Interpretation Questions

4a. What does this story teach us about faith?

4b. What can we learn from the faith of those who asked Jesus to help the woman?

5a. How does Jesus' healing reveal his authority?

5b. What are the implications of Jesus' power over sickness?

5c. Discuss how this episode with Jesus might have affected the household of Simon.

6a. Imagine that you are the mother-in-law of Simon (a) when Jesus arrived and (b) when you were healed.

6b. What can we learn about healing from this story?

Application Questions

7a. Let's discuss how Jesus affects our ability and desire to serve.

7b. Do we believe Jesus can help people today? In what ways?

7c. Do we believe that Jesus actually performed a miracle of healing as this story depicts? If not, why not?

7d. Have you asked Jesus to enter your home? life? Why haven't we done so?

Evaluation

In a beginning group, this question may not be easily grasped.

This focuses attention on one particular aspect of the story and may keep the discussion from rambling.

This simple question leads into some basic issues that Luke, the author, speaks about frequently.

For a more advanced group, this kind of question may be stimulating. A beginning group may find 5c better.

The word *discuss* encourages a wide-ranging exploration of the subject, and could lead to unprofitable speculation if the leader is not alert.

The leader could ask one person to respond to both parts or have two people respond to one part each.

Don't include too many speculative lessons.

Evaluation

Not very stimulating. It needs to be cast as a question.

This question not only addresses the ability of Jesus, but our faith and confidence in him. If your group has people in it who are not Christians, a better question could be 7c.

For those who have not yet been able to build much confidence in Jesus, this question could provide a context for growth.

This type of application question can be very threatening to some individuals. But if the climate of the study is loving, it is often surprising how open the discussion following this straightforward type of question can be.

7
Leading the Discussion

The moment has arrived. The meeting begins at 7:00 and it is 6:59. Don't panic. Remember, this isn't a lecture. Your job is simply to raise questions and to moderate the discussion. You don't need to have final answers to all the questions! It is far more important to be humble, open and appreciative of all that group members contribute to the discussion.

Creating a Comfortable Setting

Before the meeting, try to create a comfortable setting for the discussion. If possible, choose a meeting room that is informal and attractive, such as a living room. Arrange the seats in a circle rather than rigid rows so people can have eye contact with each other. Make sure the room is well-lighted and the temperature is comfortable. Offer people refreshments, such as coffee, tea or soft drinks. (This can be done at the beginning or end of the meeting, or both.) Our group likes to pass around a bowl of popcorn for those who want to nibble. Have extra Bibles on hand for those who need them.

Getting Started

Begin promptly at the announced time. If you wait for people to gather, they will acquire the habit of being late. Plan the early minutes carefully so they will be interesting and profitable to those who are prompt, but not so crucial that latecomers will be hopelessly lost.

One way to deal with lateness is to announce that the group will gather at 7:00 so people can hang up their coats and get a cup of coffee. But also tell everyone ahead of time that the study itself will begin at 7:15. Then be sure to start the discussion promptly at the announced time.

Getting Acquainted

Make sure everyone knows each other. When group members are open with each other and relaxed in personal relationships, dynamic discussion and effective learning usually take place. When members are uneasy with one another, both the discussion and the learning process are hindered. After those present have been introduced to one another, address people by name to help others remember names.

Begin with Prayer

Begin the meeting with prayer. Ask God to help each of you to understand and apply the passage. If you ask someone else to pray, be sure he or she is informed prior to the study, as some people are unaccustomed to praying in a group. It is usually best to leave group prayer until the end of the discussion.

Read the Passage

After giving an introduction to the study and asking an approach question, read the passage aloud if you are studying one chapter or less. You may choose to do this yourself or someone else may read. But remember that some people are embarrassed to read aloud in public, especially when threatened with obscure names or theological terms. If you ask several people to read, paragraphs make sensible units. Usually the practice of having each person read only one verse breaks the continuity of the passage.

When you study a historical narrative, such as those found in the Gospels and Acts, it is sometimes fun to read them dramatically. Assign parts for the various characters in the story. This can bring a passage to life and give you a sense of being there.

Encourage the members of the group to use a contemporary translation of the Bible rather than a paraphrase. The New International Version, the New American Standard Bible and the Revised Standard Version are recommended. The King James Version is beautifully written but is sometimes difficult to understand.

Principles of Good Leadership

Good leaders are facilitators. They strike the match which ignites the group—primarily by affirming the members of the group and encouraging them to participate. There are several principles which, if followed, will enable you to be an effective leader.

1. Your attitude as the leader is one of the most significant factors in determining the spirit and tone of the discussion. Your respect for the authority of the Bible will be contagious even though you may never express it in words. Your love and openness toward people in the group will quickly infect those around you. Your relaxed attitude and genuine enjoyment of the discussion will spread to every group member from the start of the discussion.

2. At the beginning of your first time together, explain that these studies are meant to be discussions not lectures. Then read or summarize the following guidelines for Bible discussions:

a. The Bible is our textbook. We should let the Bible speak for itself rather than depending on what we have heard or read about it.

b. Stick to the passage being studied. Our answers should be based on the verses which are the focus of the discussion.

c. Realize that each person's part in the discussion helps us to learn. Participate freely, but allow others to also.

3. If the study guide has an introductory paragraph, read or summarize this for the group. This will orient the group to the passage being studied.

4. As you begin to ask the group the questions in the guide, it will be helpful to keep several things in mind. First, the questions can often be used just as they are written. If you wish, you may simply read them aloud to the group. Or you may prefer to express them in your own words. However, unnecessary rewording of the questions is not recommended.

5. There may be times when it is appropriate to deviate from the study guide. For example, a question may have already been answered. If so, move on to the next question. Or someone may raise an important question not covered in the guide. Take time to discuss it! The important thing is to use discretion. There may be many routes you can travel to reach the goal of the study. But the easiest route is usually the one the author has suggested.

6. Avoid answering your own questions. If necessary, repeat or rephrase the question until it is clearly understood. An eager group quickly becomes passive and silent if they think the leader will do most of the talking.

7. Don't be afraid of silence. People need time to think about the question before formulating their answers. But try to discern the difference between fruitful silence (when people are thinking) and blanks (when your question seems unclear or irrelevant).

8. Don't be content with just one answer. Additional contributions will usually add depth and richness to the discussion. Ask, "What do the rest of you think?" or "Anything else?" until several people have had a chance to speak.

9. Be affirming! People will contribute much more eagerly if they feel their answers are genuinely appreciated. One way to be affirming is to listen attentively whenever anyone speaks. Another is to verbally acknowledge their contribution. Respond to their answers by saying,

"That's a good observation" or "Excellent point." Be especially affirming to shy or hesitant members of the group.

10. Be willing to admit your own ignorance or faults. It is easy for leaders to feel that they must have answers to all questions raised. If a wrong answer is given, or if a leader makes a mistake and fails to admit it, community spirit will be hindered. Admitting our faults and weaknesses will often release the entire group to a new level of openness to God's grace and to one another.

11. Periodically summarize what the *group* has said about the passage. This helps to draw together the various ideas mentioned and gives continuity to the study. But don't preach.

12. Conclude your time together with conversational prayer. Give everyone who wants to pray an opportunity to pray. Ask God's help to apply those things which you learned in the study.

13. Be sure to end on time. There is always a temptation to allow the study to continue. But if the group has previously decided to begin and end at a certain time, you should respect their decision. Studies that regularly go beyond the agreed time limit will tend to be counterproductive. Better to leave the group desiring more from the Scriptures than wishing they had less!

Handling Problems

Problems may arise in any discussion. If they are handled properly, however, they need not hurt the quality of the study.

What do you do, for example, if someone tries to monopolize the discussion? You might respond by saying, "Why don't we find out what some of the others think?" You might also direct your next question to those who have not been able to participate: "Why don't we hear from those who haven't spoken yet?" If the problem persists, try talking with the person privately after the study. Help the person to understand the importance of balanced participation. Ask for his or her help in drawing out the more quiet members of the group.

How should you respond to answers which are blatantly wrong? You should never simply reject an answer. If it is obviously wrong, you could ask, "Which verse led you to that conclusion?" Or let the group handle the problem. Ask, "What do the rest of you think about this?" Their response will usually be sufficient for clearing up the misunderstanding.

What about controversy? Actually, controversy can be very stimulating! Allow people to share their thoughts freely. If you don't resolve an issue completely, move on and keep it in mind for later. A subsequent study may solve the problem.

What if the group goes off on a tangent? Encourage people to return to the passage under consideration. It should be the source for answering questions. Unnecessary cross-referencing should also be avoided.

Don't ignore problems. Deal with them in the group or in private, but do deal with them. Confronting one another in love requires God's grace and wisdom. But if someone is regularly frightening off new Christians or continually harangues the group with his or her own pet ideas, action may be needed. Always communicate acceptance of the person but realize that if nothing is done, the group could wither and die.

Following the suggestions given in this chapter should help you lead an enjoyable and profitable discussion. But leading a study should also be a *learning* experience for you. Even the most effective leader can always find room for improvement! It is helpful, therefore, to evaluate the study and your leadership once the discussion has concluded. This is the subject of the next chapter.

Basic Rules

1. *The Bible is our textbook.*
The primary purpose of the discussion is to discover together what the Bible says. Opinions of group members, though welcomed, are not the main focal points. Nor are the pronouncements of favorite pastors or authors, commentators or pollsters. Let the Bible speak for itself!

2. *What does this passage say?*
The main goal is to understand the clear teaching of the text of Scripture chosen for each study. Although some group members may have a grasp of what many other passages of the Bible say about the theme, the focus of the discussion should be the chosen text. This enables the group to carefully search the text and frees even the novice or newcomer to participate. Even internationals from non-Christian religions who have never opened a Bible are able to make valuable contributions at the first Bible study they attend.

3. *Questions are the key.*
As a key unlocks a door, a question unlocks the mind of group members so they are able to listen to what the Bible says. They direct attention, focus a group's interest and prepare a context for response. The discussion which follows a well-placed question will enrich the entire group.

4. *Leave reference works at home.*
Although commentaries are of great value in the personal study and preparation of both leader and members, they have no place in the study group. If a member brings a commentary, it, rather than the Bible, tends to be the final authority.

5. *Foster group ownership.*
The healthiest group Bible studies are those in which all participants consider the study theirs. Invitations of "Come to our study," rather than "Come to Jane's study," are a sign that members have a sense of ownership. Generally, members who consider the study theirs will contribute more responsibly, prepare more thoroughly, invite others more freely, and pray for the study more faithfully.

6. *Keep the group small.*
An ideal Bible study group includes eight to ten people. If the group experiences growth, as well-led groups usually do, members should consider dividing into two groups when there are more than twelve people. In the smaller groups, each member will have an opportunity for more frequent participation. To make a successful division, prepare carefully and openly well in advance. Groom additional leaders who will have an opportunity to lead the group before the split so that those who will be joining that leader's group will be acquainted with him or her. If space allows, some groups avoid the trauma of separation by meeting together in a common place and then splitting into different groups for the study. Others occasionally reassemble to share what God has been teaching them, thus keeping ties with the original members.

8
Evaluating the Discussion

Agood small group Bible study is like a popcorn popper. At first there are only a few pops as one or two people warm up to the group. Pretty soon, however, there is an explosion of sound as everyone begins to comment.

A poor Bible study is like a popcorn popper with a damaged heater. The group never warms up. Awkward silences are broken only occasionally by a cough or a lifeless, one-word answer.

What makes the difference between a good Bible study and a poor one? The three most important ingredients are the leader, the group and the questions. This chapter will help you and your group to evaluate each of these.

The Leader
An evaluation is not a score of your performance. ("And here are the

results of the judges: 8.0, 8.5, 7.5, 7.0 and 8.0.") It is primarily a *learning* experience which helps you identify the strengths and weaknesses of your leadership so you can do even better next time. After the discussion, answer the following questions as objectively as possible. As you do so, ask God to show you any improvements or changes you need to make:

☐ Were you well prepared, having devoted a sufficient amount of time to prayer and study?

☐ Did you have a good grasp of the passage?

☐ Were you familiar with the questions and the leader's notes?

☐ Were you comfortable in your role as leader? Why or why not?

☐ Did you provide an adequate introduction to the study?

☐ Did you give people time to think about each question?

☐ Did you rephrase any unclear questions?

☐ Did you encourage more than one response to each question?

☐ Did you actively listen to each person's comments?

☐ Did you respond to these comments in an affirming manner?

☐ Did you ever answer your own question?

☐ Did you keep the discussion moving at a proper pace?

☐ Did you handle problems effectively?

☐ Did you begin and end the discussion on time?

☐ What can you do to improve the quality of your leadership next time?

These questions can also help you train a new discussion leader. Give the person suggestions for leading a discussion (see chapter seven), then offer a chance to lead. Use the questions to evaluate his or her leadership after the study.

The Group

The members of the group also have an important responsibility. An eager group can make the difference between a vibrant, dynamic discussion and one which administers general anesthesia. After your group has completed a series of studies, or if the discussions tend to drag, spend a few minutes together evaluating their participation.

☐ Are the members of the group at ease with each other?

☐ Do they come to the meeting prepared?

☐ Is their participation balanced or unbalanced?

☐ Do certain members tend to dominate the discussion?

☐ Do others tend to remain silent?

☐ Are most of the answers directed to the leader or do people interact with each other freely?

☐ Do they actively listen to each other's comments?

☐ Do they respond to these comments in an affirming manner?

☐ If any problems or controversies arise, does the group handle these effectively or do they leave this to the leader?

☐ Is your meeting room comfortable and pleasant?

☐ What suggestions can the group offer for improving the quality of their participation?

The Questions

Good questions are a crowbar for the brain. They pry open our minds by causing us to think. Good questions don't guarantee you'll have a lively discussion, but they are an important ingredient. Whether you write your own questions or use a study guide, evaluate the questions from time to time. Better yet, ask one or two members of the group to evaluate them for you after the study. This will help you understand why some studies work well and others put people to sleep. (Suggestions for *improving* the quality of the questions are found in chapter six.)

☐ How would you rate the overall quality of this study in terms of interest, content and applicability?

☐ Was the introductory paragraph helpful in orienting the group to the study?

☐ If the author used an approach question (see chapter six), did it help the group to "warm up" to the topic of the study?

☐ Was the study interesting and thought provoking?

☐ Did the questions draw out the content and meaning of the passage?

□ Did they do a good job of generating discussion?

□ Were any of the questions problematic or poorly written? If so, which ones and why?

□ At the end of the study, did the group have a grasp of the central truths of the passage?

□ Did the study lead the group to apply these truths in a helpful manner?

□ Were there a proper number of questions for the amount of time the discussion was intended to last?

□ What suggestions can you offer for improving the quality of this study?

9
Growing Together

Bible discussions thrive in a context of love and mutual support. They should be enjoyable, an event that every member eagerly anticipates week by week. The apostle Paul writes, "Speaking the truth in love, we are to grow up in every way into him who is the head, into Christ" (Eph 4:15 RSV). A Bible discussion is an ideal opportunity to experience this.

How can we achieve a healthy climate in our study group? The answer is found in the book of Acts. When the church began after Pentecost they met in small groups when "they broke bread in their homes." Note how the early church functioned in this passage:

They devoted themselves to the apostles' teaching and to the fellowship, to the breaking of bread and to prayer. Everyone was filled with awe, and many wonders and miraculous signs were done by the apostles. All the believers were together and had everything in common. Selling their possessions and goods, they gave to anyone as he had need. Every day they continued to meet together in the temple courts. They broke bread in their homes and ate together with glad and sincere hearts, praising God and enjoying the favor of all the people. And the Lord added to their number daily those who were being saved. (Acts 2:42-47)

We can identify four distinct components of their life together: *nurture* ("they devoted themselves to the apostles' teaching"), *community* ("and to fellowship"), *worship* ("to the breaking of bread and to prayer") and *mission* ("they gave to anyone as he had need . . . enjoying the favor of all the people. And the Lord added to their number"). Bible study will go a long way toward meeting your group's need for nurture (feeding on the spiritual food of God's Word). But what about the other three components? Let's look at each one in turn.*

Community

The word *fellowship* originally meant to share something in common with others. It did not have an exclusively religious meaning. For example, we usually form friendships with those who have common interests, background, education, socioeconomic status and so on. These things form the basis of our "fellowship."

Yet people in the early church had few of these things in common. Slaves met with free, poor met with wealthy, young met with old, Jews met with Gentiles, and the weak met with the powerful. In the first-century culture these associations were the most unlikely imaginable! What in the world did they have in common? The answer, of course, is Jesus Christ. He was the basis of their fellowship. He welded a supernatural bond where no natural one could exist.

There is a supernatural bond among the members of your small group. As Paul says, we have "one Lord, one faith, one baptism; one God and Father of all" (Eph 4:5-6). We strengthen that bond as we

---

*For a detailed discussion of the nature and function of small groups, read *Good Things Come in Small Groups, Small Group Leaders' Handbook,* or *Getting Together* (all from IVP).

share those things which we have in common. This is the true meaning of Christian community.

Allow time for the members of your group to have fellowship with each other. For example, there can be time for informal interaction before and after the meeting. Fifteen minutes at the beginning of the meeting is usually adequate. After the meeting, encourage people to stay as long as they like (if you're not imposing on the host or hostess). This relaxed atmosphere can sometimes be enhanced by serving refreshments. People tend to be more at ease and ready to talk if they have a cup of coffee or a soft drink in their hand.

In the study itself, encourage one another. Sometimes individuals become so concerned about themselves and correct interpretations that they forget the human side of fellow members. All of us need affirmation when we have done a good job or made a valuable contribution. Both leader and members should aim to compliment at least one other person each time the group meets. And of course the leader may have many opportunities to respond affirmatively to members' remarks during the course of a discussion.

After the Bible study, ask the group if they have any prayer requests or answers to prayer they would like to share. Are they facing any difficulties or problems? Has the Lord taught them anything recently? As the group begins to experience this kind of community together, the members will be strengthened, encouraged and will learn to love each other more deeply.

Outside activities can also enhance your fellowship. Go out for pizza or ice cream. Plan a potluck supper or progressive dinner. Have a weekend retreat or picnic together. Be creative!

Worship

Fellowship with each other should lead naturally to fellowship with the Lord. Worship him together. Praise him. Sing songs or hymns together.

Worship can be directly related to the Bible study. For example, as our group studied the book of Jonah, we concluded by praising and thanking God for his compassion to Jonah, the Ninevites and us. We also sang a hymn of praise to God. Sometimes worship will happen spontaneously. But it is usually best to plan a time of worship around the theme of the study. This can be done by the leader, or someone else in the group can be in charge of that part of your time together. Also go to God with the prayer requests the group has shared. Thank him for any answers to prayer.

Some groups keep a prayer notebook. On one side of the page they write their requests and when they first prayed about them. On the opposite side of the page they record the answers to these prayers. As the group reviews these requests and answers periodically, they will be amazed at all that God has done for them.

Mission

Many groups decide to work together in some form of mission or outreach. This can be a practical way of applying what you have learned. For example, you can visit people at a home for the elderly. Help a widow with cleaning or repair jobs around her home. Support a missionary through prayer, correspondence and giving. Host a series of evangelistic discussions for your friends or neighbors. Such projects can have a transforming influence on your group.

As you look for ways to apply what you have learned, don't overlook the needs within your group. Pray for each other throughout the week. Visit those who become sick or hospitalized. Our group helped two of our members to move furniture into their new home. On another occasion we helped a couple in our group to reroof a house. Such love was costly in terms of sore muscles and smashed fingers, but we grew closer as a result. Believe it or not, it was also fun!

Your group will need to work at keeping a balance among the various components of small groups. For example, if your meeting ends at 7:30, don't wait until 7:20 to begin your sharing and prayer! A good rule of thumb is to allow fifteen minutes for informal conversation, thirty to forty-five minutes for Bible study, and thirty minutes for sharing and prayer. Once a month you might also do some form of outreach or some other outside activity together as a group.

Moving On

Our Wednesday night group was involved with each of these aspects of group life. As a result we all grew—both as individuals and as a group. We no longer meet together regularly for study. Many of us have moved on to join other small groups where we enjoy fellowship together, nurture from God's Word, worship of our Lord and outreach to those around us. But the impact and memory of our Bible study on Wednesday nights will remain with us for many years. Our hope and prayer is that you will also be part of many such groups in the years to come.

James F. Nyquist served as director of the literature department for Inter-Varsity Christian Fellowship for twenty years. He is honorary literature secretary for the International Fellowship of Evangelical Students. Jack Kuhatschek, a former staff member with Inter-Varsity Christian Fellowship, is Bible study editor for InterVarsity Press.

Appendix
A Model Study

Humility
Mark 10:32-45

P ride comes in all shapes and sizes. Some of us put ourselves on a pedestal from which we judge the faults of everyone else. Others are so self-effacing that they cannot take their eyes off themselves and their own inadequacies. Still others swing like a pendulum from one extreme to the other. Paul exhorts us neither to exalt nor to belittle ourselves, but rather to think of ourselves with sober judgment (Rom 12:3). As we read in Mark 10:32-45, the disciples too were constantly learning to walk in humility like the Lord Jesus.

Approach question

1. What is the difference between humility and a poor self-image?

Observation question

2. Read Mark 10:32-45. What does Jesus tell his disciples about what awaits him in Jerusalem (vv. 32-34)?

**Interpretation
question**
3. In light of this news, how is the request of James and John inappropriate (v. 35)?

**Application
question**
4. In what ways do you tend to be ambitious like James and John?

**Combination
observation/
interpretation
question**
5. The words *baptism* and *cup* in verses 38-39 are sometimes used symbolically in Scripture to denote suffering. In this context, explain Jesus' reply to James and John.

**Interpretation
question**
6. Compare the sin of the other ten disciples with that of James and John (v. 41).

**Application
question**
Have you ever felt envious or even indignant when others were honored and you were not? Explain.

**Observation
question**
7. How does Jesus contrast greatness in the world with greatness in God's kingdom (vv. 42-45)?

46 _____

Interpretation question   What is so radical about his definition of greatness?

Application question   **8.** In what ways do Christians today still embrace the world's concept of greatness?

Application question   **9.** Give a positive example of humility in action that you've seen in your church, family or work.

Application question   **10.** Jesus' concept of greatness and humility could transform every area of our lives. Name one way you could begin to follow his example.

This study is by Andrea Sterk and Peter Scazzero. It is from a LifeBuilder Bible Study entitled Christian Character: Becoming the Person God Wants You to Be *(Downers Grove, Ill.: InterVarsity Press, 1985), pp. 44-46.*